# WHEN GOD WHISPERS

My heart's desire is for
this book be an inspiration
in your life's journey

Tammy Schapinzeel

May 1/2016
Dear Lynne,
I will always remember the
most wonderful times we
spent with our dear brother!!!
Murray. He was one of the best!!!
much loved & dearly missed!
And he's with all his
loved ones who have
gone before him.
We'll meet again
in God's time
Love
Gwen

P.S
page 77
Dedicated poem
to Murray

# WHEN GOD WHISPERS

TAMMY SCHERPENZEEL

WESBROOK BAY BOOKS
Vancouver, B.C.

Wesbrook Bay Books

wesbrookbay@gmail.com www.facebook.com/wesbrookbay/

www.wesbrookbay.com



Cover design by Katrina Johanson

Interior design by 2 Austens

Edited by BDG

ISBN: 978-1-928112-36-5

# Contents

# Introduction

Do you know God's purpose for your life?

Just take a moment and meditate on that question.

Since time began, He has had a plan, a purpose, for each one of us. God has created everyone for a reason. I have often wondered, especially during difficult times, the reason why God breathed life into me. I have been through spiritual, emotional and physical valleys. I have struggled with not feeling God's presence in my life. I have cried till I feel there are no more tears left to fall. Afflicted with an illness. I have cried out, "why me?"

Since then I have since realized that these times strengthened me and brought me closer to Him because I heard the sweet, small whisper of God. His encouraging words lifted me to new heights. Yes, even to the mountaintops. When I stumbled, God has been there to catch and hold me in His loving arms.

Because of His great love, He gave His only Son to be crucified for me and for you. The power of His love and mercy guides me through my daily walk with Him. He has given me a vision, a purpose in my life. A vision of sharing hope and truth to others. The encouraging words whispered in my ear during my trials, He wants me to pass on to you to help you in your time of despair. At the end of every trial, there is rejoicing because of our faith in Jesus Christ, our Redeemer and friend. We are to give God the glory, honour and power through every aspect of our lives. Listen for God's whisper. He has breathed life into us for a reason. Submit to God's purpose for your life.

# At the Sound of Your Voice

Oh Lord God Almighty,
who was and is
and is to come.
God of this great universe,
and all that is within.

You spoke
and the sound of Your voice
set orbits into motion;
the galaxies–planets, suns,
moons and stars.

You spoke
and the sound of Your voice
breathed life
into all living things;
great and small.

You spoke

and the sound of Your voice
turned the desert
into pools of water;
dry land into springs.

You speak
and the sound of Your voice
parts the raging waters
so I can walk
on dry ground.

You speak
and the sound of Your voice
delivers the promises
at the moment
You command.

You speak
and the sound of Your voice
bestows power on me
to accomplish
all that You desire.

Breathe on me
Holy Spirit.
I want to hear
the sound of Your voice
as You speak to me.

Part I

# GIFTS OF GRACE and LOVE

I

# THE GREATEST GIFT

Oh God!
  Your love, so amazing.
  wraps me in
  unconditional love.
  Always with me,
  every moment of my life,
  carrying me through
  rough waters,
  setting me down safely
  on other side.
  Guiding me to light
  through dark tunnels,
  raising me up
  from deep valleys,

placing me on the mountaintop.
You rejoice with me
in my triumphs and celebrations.
Is Jesus worth living for?

Do I let You have complete control of my life?
Do I lean on You through all the hard times?
Do I thank and praise You for every blessing?
Or do I just call on You in my trials?
Do I cry out, "Where are You, Lord?
Why have You forgotten me?"
Am I worth dying for?

Help me to never forget
that Jesus is worth living for.

Jesus bore the shame, the ridicule.
He willingly wore crown of thorns
and agonized as they nailed Him on the cross.
Even through that immense pain,
His amazing love poured out.
He cried out to His Father,
"Forgive them
for they do not know what they do,"
He paid the debt for my sins,
and for yours,
giving His life as the ultimate sacrifice.

But Jesus is no longer in the ground.
He arose!
He proclaimed His love for mankind,
through His suffering, His crucifixion,
His righteousness.
He granted us the greatest gift of all.
Eternal life!
Yes, Jesus is worth living for!

*The Greatest Gift*

Ask yourself, "is Jesus worth living for? Am I worth dying for?"

Mankind has been so blessed by a marvelous gift. Sadly, not everyone realizes this. Would you sacrifice your life for your enemies, let alone your friends? Would you allow them to ridicule and taunt you?

Well, Jesus did. He gave His life to be a living sacrifice. Imagine the agony Jesus faced as He had the knowledge of what God's plan was for Him. Jesus was going to have separation from God, His Father, to die for your sins and mine. Jesus was mocked and severely beaten. A crown of thorns was placed on His head. Blood ran down His face from the thorns piercing His skull. Nails were hammered into His hands to hold Him to the cross. Not only did Jesus' blood pour out, but also His love and mercy for all mankind. Because of God's gift of eternal life for us, Jesus endured the agony of His crucifixion. But, that was not the end. There was the glorious resurrection. Death was defeated on the cross.

The gift of God's love, mercy, forgiveness and eternal life are given to those who place their faith and trust in Him. Now ask yourself, "is Jesus worth living for?"

"*But God showed His great love for us by sending Christ to die for us while we were still sinners. And since we have been made right in God's sight by the blood of Christ, He will certainly save us from God's condemnation. For since our friendship with God was restored by the death of His Son while we were still His enemies, we will certainly be saved through the life of His Son.*"

Romans 5:8-10

## 2

# THE POTTER

"You are the Potter,
I am the clay."

As the potter's wheel turns,
he skillfully
molds and shapes
the clay.
Creating his masterpiece.
So precious,
so beautiful.
God skillfully
molds and shapes me
as life unfolds.

When I become distorted
living life my way,
He does not leave me
by the wayside.
God gently picks me up.
Creating His masterpiece.

God will skillfully
mold and shape you.
Allow Him to pick you up
and lay
His loving hands
on you.
Creating His masterpiece.
So precious,
So beautiful.

Enable God to work freely with you
Molding and shaping you
As He wills.

## The Potter

I find it fascinating to observe someone enthusiastically using their talents. For example, a potter. As the wheel turns, the potter's hands skillfully and lovingly shapes the clay into a beautiful masterpiece. If the clay does not yield to the potter's hands, the potter just picks it up and starts over. Once the creation has been moulded and shaped, the potter then puts it in a furnace to strengthen the object. So it is in our lives. God is the Potter and we are His clay. God adds Living Water and gently pulls us up and forms us into His special creation. When we become distorted, He doesn't give up on us, but He picks us up and keeps working with us to create His vessel. Through the process, God needs to place us in the furnace of life to refine and strengthen us. We are to yield to God moulding, shaping and refining us into His unique creation- a clay vessel lovingly created by the Potter, the Master of all potters.

"*All Scripture is inspired by God and is useful to teach us what is true and to make us realize what is wrong in our lives. It corrects us when we are wrong and teaches us to do what is right. God uses it to prepare and equip His people to do every good work.*"

2 Timothy 3:16-17

# 3

# BREATH OF LIFE

Thank you Almighty God
for Your written Word.
I search Your scriptures
seeking guidance,
absorbing knowledge of
Your laws, teachings, and truths.
Fill me with wisdom
to do Your will.
Have Your Holy Spirit
live within me.

Thank You Sovereign Lord
for Your written Word.
I listen to Your voice,

seeking Your instruction.
I walk in faith and wisdom of
listening, trusting, and obeying You.
Feeling renewed, refreshed
doing Your will.
Every breath I take,
I breathe in You.

Thank You merciful God
for Your written Word.
I follow Your leading,
seeking to do Your will.
Your great mercy saturates me with
love, peace, and grace.
Fill me with wisdom
to help others.
My heart's desire is to
live and breathe the written Word.

## Breath of Life

The minister of our church challenged the congregation to read through the bible chronologically in one year. I took part in that challenge. Each Sunday, our minister preached on points, aspects, and truths of life's lessons that God would have us learn through His Word. One of the many truths that stuck in my mind was that whenever someone followed God's will, they were protected and escaped harm. When I was engulfed with the reading of His Word, I learned to rely on Him and He would see me through whatever came my way. I was lifted by God's security, but I also felt His wrath because of my guilt. God gave me the wisdom to realize my many faults, but He also reminded me of the assurance of knowing His grace and mercy and His redeeming power of His shed blood. He not only filled me with His peace, but He filled my heart with a desire to live and breathe the written Word.

*"But you must remain faithful to the things you have been taught. You know they are true, for you know you can trust those who taught you. You have been taught the Holy Scriptures from childhood, and they have given you the wisdom to receive the salvation that comes by trusting in Christ Jesus. All Scripture is inspired by God and is useful to teach us what is true and to make us realize what is wrong in our lives. It corrects us when we are wrong and teaches us to do what is right. God uses it to prepare and equip His people to do every good work."*

2 Timothy 3:14-17

# 4

# THE NEW BIRTH

A new day.
A new season.
Rustling, vibrant leaves
fall.
Rich, beautiful flowers
wither.
Luscious, green grass
fades.
The beauty of nature
sleeps.
God provides protection,
a blanket of snow.

A new season.

A new birth.
The trees' tiny buds
open.
The flowers' colourful petals
blossom.
The green grass
flourishes.
The beauty of nature
awakens.
God has performed
another miracle.

A new birth.
A new life.
I have been reborn
by the grace of God.
As snow's moisture
seeps into ground,
His Holy Spirit's moisture
saturates me.
He cleanses me
white as snow.
God provides protection
by His righteousness.

A new season.
A new birth.
A new life.

God's new creation!

## The New Birth

In God's creation, each season has a purpose. In autumn, the leaves fall, the flowers die off and the green grass turns brown. Everything becomes dormant. Dead. Wintertime is a wonderful season which God has created for a reason. I always anticipate that first snowfall. I enjoy seeing the snow flurries lightly falling and covering the deadness. Just envision how peaceful and tranquil the scene. God protects nature with each snowfall. A blanket of snow is it's covering. In the spring there is newness of life. Grass becomes green. Buds appear on the trees and the flowers come alive with their blossoms. All as a result of the snow's moisture which God provided. In everyone's life, there are seasons as well. Through the knowledge and acceptance of our Lord Jesus Christ who sacrificed His life for each one of us, our old selves die to the world. God offers us protection with His righteousness. He cleanses us from all sin and we become as white as snow. We are reborn by the grace of God. Our inner being is transformed into something beautiful. During summer, our season of growth, we are strengthened by our faith in our Creator. He will do a marvelous work in us and through us. We have become His new creation.

*"Since we believe that Christ died for all, we also believe that we have all died to our old life. He died for everyone so that those who receive his new*

*life will no longer live for themselves. Instead, they will live for Christ, who died and was raised for them....This means that anyone who belongs to Christ has become a new person. The old life is gone; a new life has begun!"*

2 Corinthians 5:14-17

5

# A BLESSING

A precious miracle.
God's gift to us.
Entrusting us
to your care.
Rejoicing,
cradling you
in our arms.
Face of an angel.
Warmth of your smile
brings sunshine
into our lives.
Sparkle of your eyes
brightens even

the darkest days.
You are the rainbow
amongst the clouds.
Rivers of life overflow
with your caring,
loving kindness.
Growing in God's love,
filling you with His peace.
Providing you with
wisdom and strength.
Reaching the mountaintop.
Becoming as strong and mighty
as the wind.
You share your
love, compassion and strength
with others.
Blessing those with
providing your love,
your knowledge of God.
We will forever be
together through eternity;
one of God's promised blessings.

## A Blessing

Children are blessings from God. The birth of a child is one of

God's greatest miracles. As I was growing up, I always imagined myself having many children. I had visions of the table at mealtime being surrounded with a large family. But what we have planned is not always God's plan. My dream of a large family ended when a physical problem became a part of my life. The specialist informed me I would never be able to have children, because it could be a danger to me as well as my child. But, God's power is greater! My husband and I were blessed with one of God's greatest miracles; the birth of a beautiful baby boy. I thank God and praise Him every day for His wonderful blessing. I decided to write this poem for David. It took me a few years to write as I watched him grow up to be a very mature young man who loves the Lord. I know that God is using David for His purpose. Every child is a gift from God. Each one is unique in his or her own way. They are not all perfect, but all children are talented even though they may have mental and physical disabilities. They will shine with their talents if we enable God to work in and through them. God entrusts children to our care and blesses us with His miracles; but, God not only blesses parents with His miracles, He also blesses the childless by entrusting the care of some children to them. Every child is one of God's miracles. Thank Him for His blessings.

"*Children are a gift from the Lord; they are a reward from Him.*"

Psalm 127:3

6

# THE KING'S CHILD

At the feet of Jesus
I come,
as a child
of the King.
*Listening.*
*Trusting.*
*Obeying.*
*Rejoicing*
in His love.

The King's Child

Do you ever wish you were a part of royalty? Well you don't have to make that wish anymore, because you are! You are a child of a King. The most magnificent King past, present and future. He is not the King of a country, but He is the King of the universe. God, the King, is an all-powerful, all-loving and an all-knowing King, your Heavenly Father. He is never too busy to have you, as one of His children, come to Him and sit at His feet. He is a God of forgiveness if you come to Him repenting of your sins and lay them at His feet. Your Heavenly Father is always listening as you talk with Him seeking His advice. Listen for God's small whisper as He speaks to you. Be obedient to His guidance by putting your faith and trust in Him. He will embrace you with His loving arms as you praise and thank Him for His many blessings which He has given to you. Remember the times when your earthly parents stood by the side lines as you played sports and cheered you on. Well your Heavenly Father is there to cheer you on in life and rejoice with you in all your accomplishments. Not only is He with you in your successes, but He is also there to sustain you in your failures. As you know, we all deal with them. But, what a comfort to know that the King, our Heavenly Father, is there with us if we are obedient to His will. We, as a child of the King, can rejoice in His Fatherly love.

"*And I will be your Father, and you will be my sons and daughters, says the Lord Almighty.*"

2 Corinthians 6:18

Part II

# REPENTANCE and DELIVERANCE

7

# BREAKING FREE

Oh Lord, hear my cries.
My heart, full
with sadness,
pours my heart out
to You.
For You are
the all-knowing God.

Tears flow
from my listless eyes —
eyes full of darkness.
I lift them in search of
Your light.
For You are

the all-knowing God.

You see my anguish although
my lips utter no sound.
I am silent,
yet,
You hear me.
For You are
the all-knowing God.

Oh Lord, You have heard my cries.
Filled my heart with gladness.
Your light shines through my eyes.
You have opened my mouth with song.
You have raised me up to sing Your praises.
For You are
the all-knowing God.

## Breaking Free

There are times in my life, as in everyone's life, that I feel I am at my lowest point.

I have hit bottom. I just cannot carry on. All of my strength is gone. There is no reason to continue with life. I feel God has deserted me and there is darkness all around me. I fall on my knees and cry out to God seeking His presence. I struggle to pray, but no words come. Overcome with frustration and already distraught, I fail at any attempt to pray. But then, I hear a small whisper in my ear reminding me that God Himself knows everything. He knows what is on my heart and on my mind.

God doesn't need to hear the words because He hears my heart and knows my thoughts at all times. He has heard my cries and I rejoice because He is with me. God is always with me wherever I am in my life emotionally and spiritually. Remember at those difficult times in your life, that God is there to lift us up if we cry out to Him and seek His help. Yes, even when we are silent, He still hears us. God is our Deliverer. We can rejoice and sing praises to Him, for God is an all-knowing God.

*"And the Holy Spirit helps us in our weakness .... the Holy Spirit prays for us with groaning that cannot be expressed in words. And the Father who knows all hearts knows what the Spirit is saying, for the Spirit pleads for us believers in harmony with God's own will. And we know that God causes everything to work together for the good of those who love God and are called according to His purpose for them."*

Romans 8:26-28

# 8

# CALVARY

O gracious Lord and Saviour.

Praise to Your Holy Name!
  I give You thanks.
  Because of Your precious blood
  shed for me,
  I have been set free.

  I was trapped
  under the bondage of sin.
  With my transgressions,
  I came to You.
  Falling on my knees.
  Broken and guilt-ridden.

You stretched out Your arms,
revealing Your nail-pierced hands.
You lovingly said,
"I love you this much.
Your sins have been forgiven.
I have set you free."

You have rescued me.
Because of Your abundant
grace and mercy,
my sins have gone.
Washed away.
Forgiven and forgotten.

The chains have disappeared.

## Calvary

The heaviness of guilt has been a weight bearing down on my shoulders. Trapped, I have lived in such darkness that it hindered my ability to feel God's grace and mercy so freely given to everyone.

I felt separated from God's love. Don't misunderstand me. God has never stopped loving me, but I felt I didn't deserve His love. Picture yourself looking up and seeing Jesus with His arms opened wide revealing His nail pierced hands and saying "I love you this much!"

What an awesome vision! Because of His shed blood and His love for each one of us, the weight has been lifted from our shoulders. I praise and thank my Saviour for removing the chains and setting me free. God not only forgives our sins, but He also forgets them and washes them away. All because of His love which He demonstrated at Calvary.

*"I have swept away your sins like a cloud. I have scattered your offenses like the morning mist. Oh, return to Me, for I have paid the price to set you free."*

Isaiah 44:22

# 9

# THE LIVING SACRIFICE

Besieged by darkness.
Broken and guilt-ridden.
I am alone.
Filled with despair.
Held captive by
the bondage of sin.

I cry out to You,
merciful and loving God.
Repenting.
Because of Your
marvelous grace,
I am free.

Overwhelmed by brightness.
Restored and raised-up.
I am not alone.
Filled with hope.
I rejoice.
I am pardoned.

You are my Deliverer,
the Living Sacrifice.
Because of Your precious blood
which You shed for me,
I am redeemed from
the bondage of sin.

## The Living Sacrifice

Have you ever felt so overwhelmed with guilt?

I have. We all have if we are honest with ourselves.

I have felt trapped in a room from which I could not escape. Held captive by the heaviness of guilt. Darkness surrounded me. Crying out to God, I prayed for my deliverance from darkness into light with the knowledge of His mercy, love and forgiveness. Repenting of my sins, I looked up and observed an opening. The sun's rays beamed through. I realized it was not the sun's rays, but God's Light. By His great power, He has rescued me. God has drawn me back to Himself and has wiped away my tears and relieved me of my fears. Because of confessing and repenting of my sins, God has forgiven me through His grace and mercy. Jesus paid the penalty for my sins through His shed blood.

The door opened and brightness encased me. I have been freed from the bondage of sin. When we place our faith and trust in Him, God forgives us of our sins through our repentance. Jesus is our Deliverer from sin's bondage and He is our Redeemer. Praise His Holy Name for He is the Living Sacrifice.

*"He has rescued us from the kingdom of darkness and transferred us into the Kingdom of His dear Son who purchased our freedom and forgave our sins."*

Colossians 1:13

Part III

# GUIDANCE of THE HOLY SPIRIT

10

# THE CHOICE

My heart is heavy.
Blackness encompasses me.
Hope is gone.
Falling on knees,
earnestly praying.
I pray to One
who knows my innermost being,
my Heavenly Father and Redeemer.
I seek out choice
He desires for me.
My heart is thankful.
Light filters through.
Hope is restored.
Rising up

I am blessed.
I thank my Saviour
who has rescued me,
my Heavenly Father and Redeemer.
I survey choice,
He has set for me.

My heart is joyful.
Assurance overwhelms me.
Hope is renewed.
Standing firm,
I rejoice
in His love.
The One who loves unconditionally,
my Heavenly Father and Redeemer.
I surrender to choice,
He intends for me.
My heart is light.
Brightness surrounds me.
My hope is in You.
Following You,
I submit
to Your will.
The One who has planned my life,
my Heavenly Father and Redeemer.
I am strengthened by choice,
You have designed for me.

## The Choice

Life is made up of choices because God has given us free will. Whether we make the right or wrong choice, is up to us. When we make the wrong choices, life at that moment will seem very dark and we will have heavy hearts. The weight will be on our shoulders. Believe me, everyone has made wrong choices in their lives. Fortunately, we have the assurance that we can go to our Heavenly Father. He knows everything about us. God recognizes our thoughts, our hearts and our desires. If we ask for His help, we will be blessed with His Light shining on us. Even though we do not deserve God's grace, He willingly grants us peace and forgiveness if we come to Him. He is a God of deliverance and restoration. We are to seek the choice which is God's plan for our lives. When we make the right choices, He will fill us with His Holy Spirit. We are to surrender to the life He has planned for us. God will give us the strength to follow Him wherever He leads us and the wisdom to seek and submit to the choice He has designed for each one of us. Be receptive to God's choice for your life and He will guide you with His Light.

"*We can make our plans, but the Lord determines our steps.*"
Proverbs 16:9

"*Fix your thoughts on what is true, and honourable, and right, and pure, and lovely, and admirable. Think about things that are excellent and worthy of praise. Keep putting into practice all you learned and received from Me-everything you heard from Me and saw Me doing. Then the God of peace will be with you.*"
Philippians 4:8-9

11

# LIFE'S ROAD

Walking along life's road,
a fork in my path
lies before me.
I seek His presence.
Searching
for His light.

Drawing near to Him,
He lights my path,
directing me.
I am in His presence.
Listening
to His voice.

Walking with Him
along the path,
He leads me.
I rejoice in His presence.
Following
in His footsteps.

He fills my soul
with hope,
wisdom,
strength.

## Life's Road

Have you ever come to a fork in the road and wondered which way to go? I have and temptation has revealed its presence in front of me. It can be very appealing. Sometimes, I have yielded to that temptation. At the fork in the road, the one way is wide and has many "perks". Many, including me, have taken that path, but the path is overshadowed with darkness. The other way is less travelled, but the way is bright. So it is on our life's road. When we go down the wrong path, we are to return to the fork in the road. We are to search for His Light. Ask God for His guidance and direction. He will fill us with strength and wisdom to follow His footsteps leading us along the right path. The reward will be greater than what we can ever imagine if we follow the right road in life.

*"My child, listen to me and do as I say, and you will have a long, good life. I will teach you wisdom's ways and lead you in straight paths. When you walk, you won't be held back; when you run, you won't stumble...My child, pay attention to what I say. Listen carefully to my words. Don't lose sight of them. Let them penetrate deep into your heart, for they bring life to those who find them and healing to their whole body. Guard your heart above all else, for it determines the course of your life. Avoid all perverse talk; stay away from corrupt speech. Look straight ahead, and fix your eyes on what lies before you. Mark out a straight path for your feet; stay on the safe path. Don't get sidetracked; keep your feet from following evil."*

Proverbs 4 10-12, 20-27

12

# THE PATHWAY

Direct my paths, O God.

My eyes perceive
Your glory.
I stand in reverence
of You.

I feel Your presence.

I gaze upon
splendour of
Your mighty hand.
Sparkling stars dance
across midnight sky,

illuminating path
You have set for me.

I feel Your comfort.

You are the stars.
The moon.
The Light in darkness.
Peace in troubled world.
The One who lifts me when
I stumble.

I feel Your guidance.

## The Pathway

My husband and I both love woodworking. Creating something beautiful out of plain boards is very gratifying. The wintertime is the only season we can enjoy our hobby because we are kept busy with farm work during the other seasons. One night after we did the barn chores and the animals were all settled in, we did some work in our workshop. One beautiful moonlit night, we finished up for the evening. It was a crisp, still night and the snow was sparkling. As we were walking along our stone walkway to the house, I looked up and what a sight to behold. I stood in amazement and gazed up at the thousands of twinkling stars and the bright moon. I thought how majestic our God is. He is the Creator of this great universe. He made the moon and the stars. Even in the darkness, He gives us light. I felt so much at peace because of the knowledge He is always by my side. What a comforting thought! When I feel troubled, I just need to trust in Him knowing that He will guide and protect me. He lights the path that leads me to where I am to be. Let God be your guiding light to direct you along the path that He wills for you.

"...*I will brighten the darkness before them and smooth out the road ahead of them. Yes, I will indeed do these things; I will not forsake them.*"

Isaiah 42:16

13

# MY WALK WITH JESUS

Walking the narrow pathway,
stretching before me.
Hand in hand
with Jesus.
Ever by my side.
My friend.

Warmth of gentle breeze
whispering.
His sweet, calm voice
assuring me,
I am His.
My comforter.

In the quietness of His Spirit,
seek peaceful solitude.
Refreshes my soul.
Birds sweetly chirping,
uniting us in song.
My peacemaker.

When tempted, led astray,
searching, longing
for desires beckoning me,
hear the roar of His mighty voice.
Fierce as a lion.
My counselor.

In stillness of night,
He calls me,
leading me back home.
Once again, walking
hand in hand with Jesus.
My friend.

## My Walk With Jesus

One of my favourite songs is "In The Garden". As I go about my daily routine, I often sing the words to this great song. I also very much enjoy walking down the laneway to the back of the farm which my husband and I own. It is so peaceful. It is a refreshing time of restoring my soul. Conversing with Jesus and feeling His presence is inspiring. I develop a great friendship with Jesus when

I include Him in all my experiences which He calls each and every one of us to do. Our best friend is the one we confide in. What a privilege it is to be able to have Jesus as our best friend. Jesus needs to be in our every activity, every problem and in our every thought. In life, we will be led astray through temptation. Because of our friendship with Jesus, He will guide us back to where He wants us to be. We are to be faithful to Him. I rejoice in the knowledge that I can walk hand in hand with Jesus, my best friend.

In The Garden

*I come to the garden alone,*
*While the dew is still on the roses,*
*And the voice I hear falling on my ear*
*The Son of God discloses.*
*And He walks with me, and He talks with me,*
*And He tells me I am His own;*
*And the joy we share as we tarry there,*
*None other has ever known.*
*He speaks, and the sound of His voice*
*Is so sweet the birds hush their singing,*
*And the melody that He gave to me*
*Within my heart is ringing.*

*Charles A. Miles*

14

# THE ALPHA AND THE OMEGA

Oh Lord, Most High,
You are the Alpha.
From the beginning,
You have had a purpose
for my existence.
Every breath I take
is because of You.
My life is in
Your mighty hand.

You are my compass.
May You give me
the strength and the courage
to follow

wherever You lead me.
I seek Your guidance.

Trusting
in You alone,
to the end.
Oh Lord, Most High,

You are the Omega.

## The Alpha and The Omega

God is the beginning, the alpha, of all existence, wisdom and power. He created the heavens, the earth and all living things. He even created mankind for a purpose. God orchestrated His plan for each one of us before we were even born. He knew He was going to form us into existence before time began. What a realization! Every breath and every step I take is because of my Saviour. As you know, a compass directs you to where you need to be. In my travel on earth, God is my compass. If I have it pointed in the right direction, He leads me along the path I am to take. He gives me the wisdom and the strength to walk daily with Him. He is the God of all power and of all wisdom. Seek God and trust Him to be your compass too. He will guide me to the end even into eternity and He will do the same for you if you know Him personally. He is the Beginning and the End, the Alpha and the Omega.

*"Even before I was born, God chose me and called me by His marvelous grace. Then it pleased Him to reveal His Son to me so that I would proclaim the Good News about Jesus."*

Galations 1:15, 16.

*"Look, I am coming soon, bringing my reward with me to repay all people according to their deeds. I am the Alpha and the Omega, the First and the Last, the Beginning and the End."*

Revelation 22:12-13

Part IV

# REFUGE and STRENGTH

15

# ARMS OF JESUS

My eyes are closed.
I cannot see.
My mind is shut.
I cannot think.
There is no hope,
no peace.
Overcome with sadness.

But now,
I rejoice.
Because
at this moment,
there is assurance.
His radiant light shines down.

His Heavenly breeze
breathes on me.

My eyes are open.
I can see.
Mind is clear.
I can think.
There is hope,
is peace.
Overjoyed with gladness.

I am comforted
by His love.
I am safe
and secure.
Cradled in
the arms of Jesus.
I am His,
He is mine.

## Arms of Jesus

Do you feel like you are a nobody? Do you ever say to yourself "Why was I born? Why did I wake up this morning? Nothing in life matters." I'm sure it has crossed everyone's mind at one point or another. I'll be honest with you, I have experienced those times. At a difficult time in my life, I was surrounded in darkness. I couldn't think and comprehension was non-existent. I was overcome with sadness and loneliness. But then realization struck. These emotions can be conquered because I am a child of God. Remember as a child how comforting it was to have your parents wrap their loving arms around you? The sense of safety and security was overwhelming. It is the same way with God as we are His children. He cradles us in His everlasting arms. At those times when all hope is gone and you are filled with despair, remember God is there if you seek Him. He will cradle you in His loving arms. God will take away the despair and give you peace and abundant joy. He will fill you with renewed hope. Rejoice for the arms of Jesus are always open to receive those who come to Him.

"*Those who live in the shelter of the Most High will find rest in the shadow of the Almighty...He alone is my refuge, my place of safety; He is my God, and I trust Him. For He will rescue you from every trap and protect you from deadly disease. He will cover you with His feathers. He will shelter you with His wings. His faithful promises are your armour and protection...If you make the Lord your refuge, if you make the Most High your shelter, no evil will conquer you. For He will order His angels to protect you wherever you go. They will hold you up with their hands so you won't even hurt your foot on a stone...The Lord says, 'I will rescue those who love me. I will protect those who trust in my name. When they call on me, I will answer; I will be with them in trouble. I will rescue and honour them...I will give them My salvation'.*"

Psalm 91

# 16

# BECAUSE OF YOU

I cry out to You, Lord.
Hurting and bruised inside.
Tears flow.
My heart is heavy.
I am lifeless.
Strength is no more.
  I lift my face heavenward.
Dark clouds drift apart
revealing blue sky.
Your light shines through.
I am alive.
Strengthened by Your glory.
  I feel Your arms surround me.
Your promise to be ever present

fills me with peace.
Renews my strength.
I am alive.
Empowered by Your protection.
 I sense Your Spirit.
Your righteous armour protects my heart.
Power of Your love
enables me to stand firm.
I am reborn.
Protected by Your marvelous grace.
 All because of You.

## Because of You

There have been times when I have become emotionally distraught. Daggers pierce my soul. I will them to stop, but they continue to endanger my thoughts, my hopes and my dreams. I cry out wanting to be swallowed up by the earth. But then, realizing I belong to God, I am able to stand up strong. All because God surrounds me with His armour. He offers protection for me. When the daggers come my way, they are ricocheted by His love and grace. I no longer have to fear for God stands with me and protects my heart. If you put on the armour of righteousness, God will protect you. Remember when you are threatened by the daggers in your life, stand firm and strong and God's love will prevent them from piercing your soul. Our hearts' desires are protected all because of God's armour.

*"O God, listen to my cry! Hear my prayer! From the ends of the earth, I cry to you for help when my heart is over-whelmed. Lead me to the towering rock of safety, for you are my safe refuge, a fortress where my enemies cannot reach me. Let me live forever in your sanctuary, safe beneath the shelter of your wings! For you have heard my vows, O God. You have given me an inheritance reserved for those who fear your name. Add many years to the life of the king! May his years span the generations! May he reign under God's protection forever. May your unfailing love and faithfulness watch over him. Then I will sing praises to your name forever as I fulfill my vows each day."*

Psalm 61

17

# REJOICE!

Rejoice!

Rejoice! For the Lord is good.
His love never fails.
He stands by me in
times of adversity.
God lifts my burdens when
I cry out to Him.
He watches over me in
my failures.
God forgives me when
I fall on my knees before Him
asking for His forgiveness.
God is my refuge,

my strength.
He grants me peace.

I have been redeemed through
the cleansing power of
the precious blood of Jesus.

I am His.

## Rejoice!

I have been faced with many trials in my life and I realize many of you have as well. Worrisome can overwhelm me. I admit, many times I have tried to solve problems my way and have failed. Other times, I have been concerned about how things are going to go or how I am going to get through a certain circumstance to the point of dread. Sometimes at the end of it all, there has been no reason for concern. I have made myself sick for no reason. I rejoice because of God's grace. I have been given the wisdom and the knowledge that I can lean on Him and He grants me the assurance of always being with me. All I need to do is stop and pray. As He states in His Word, "Be still and know that I am God." He is the Almighty and All-Powerful God. There is no other power greater than that of our Lord and Saviour. He is with me and walking me through the hard times giving me the strength to carry on. Our Lord and Saviour has an unfailing love to all those who believe on Him. Rejoice and give God all the glory and honour because of His redeeming power.

*"Don't worry about anything; instead, pray about everything. Tell God what you need, and thank Him for all He has done. Then you will experience God's peace, which exceeds anything we can understand. His peace will guard your hearts and minds as you live in Christ Jesus."*

Philippians 4:6-7

18

# REFRESH ME, O LORD

In the vastness of
Your universe,
I seek
Your presence.
Abiding safely in
Your haven of rest.

Alone
with You.

I lift my face.
I stretch out my arms
feeling Your gentle breeze,
filling me with

Your peace,
Your love.

I am refreshed by
Your Holy Spirit.
You have breathed in me
new hope,
new passion.

You have strengthened me,
to accomplish all that
You want me to accomplish.
To be all
You want me to be.

## Refresh Me, O Lord

My son and I enjoy venturing out on trails, especially at Algonquin Park. On many occasions after a very vigorous climb, we reach the top of a mountain. What beauty stretches out before us. We just stand in awe as we overlook miles of majestic scenery. What a marvelous God, the Creator, we have. On one such walk, we were in a valley. We stood at the edge of a bush and gazed on a tranquil setting. A wonderful sense of peace fell over me. I thought even in these "small pockets" of God's great universe, He still sees me and am aware of where I am. God breathed on me love, hope and peace. He has given me a passion and the strength to pursue it. God refreshes my soul. Wherever you are in your life, know God is with you. He is with you in the valleys and on the mountaintops. He will offer you comfort and rest if You ask Him. God will fill your heart with love, hope and peace. He will fill you with the knowledge of His purpose for your life. God will provide you with the strength and the wisdom to accomplish all that He desires for you. Be obedient to God's plan and He will refresh your soul.

*"Wait on the Lord; be of good courage, and He shall strengthen your heart; wait, I say, on the Lord!"*

Psalm 27:14

*"The Lord will work out His plans for my life-for Your faithful love, O Lord, endures forever. Don't abandon me, for You made me."*
Psalm 138:8

19

# BEACON OF LIGHT

All alone
in sea of life.
Weary, exhausted.
Stormy,
gale winds.
Overpowered by
raging torrent.
Flailing.
Being pulled under.
Surrounded by
darkness.
Glimpsing up,
perceiving
a light shining.

I'm drawn to
beacon of light.
On solid rock.
A calm
in the storm.
Safe and secure.
God is my Lighthouse.
My refuge,
my strength
in sea of life.
Not alone!

## Beacon of Light

I love lighthouses and I realize many of you do as well. They are a comforting sight; a place of safety and security. In the dark of night, the beacon of light shines beckoning a sailor to warmth and contentment. Even in the raging waters and in times of distress when we feel we are going down for the last time, safety can be attainable. Lighthouses provide rest for a troubled soul. Our Lord and Saviour is our Lighthouse. He is the Light in times of difficulty and He beckons us to come to Him. He also reaches out to us and grasps our hand and draws us to Himself. We can seek refuge in God and He will give us the strength to tread safely in the rough waters. Because of our Lord and Saviour, our Lighthouse, we are never alone. The beacon of light can always be visible in our sea of life if we keep our eyes focused on our Lighthouse.

*"I am the light of the world. If you follow me, you won't have to walk in darkness, because you will have the light that leads to life."*
*John 12:8*

*"The Lord is my light and my salvation so why should I be afraid? The Lord is my fortress, protecting me from danger, so why should I tremble?"*
*Psalm 27:1*

*"The Lord keeps watch over you as you come and go, both now and forever."*
Psalm 121:8

20

# GOD, MY COMFORTER

Discouraged, rejected
in despair.
But now,
I rejoice because
I know
God is with me.
He is my counselor, my comforter
through every trial and tribulation.

He calms.
He stills.
He is the Light
in my darkest hour.
He carries me

through the valleys.

As the potter puts his work in the furnace
to finish his masterpiece,
God sometimes puts me through the fires
to complete His.

In the midst of
the storm,
He embraces me with
His everlasting arms.
Through the raging waters,
He takes me by the hand
and holds me up.
In the depths of the valley,
He lifts me to the
highest mountaintop.

My eyes focus on Him.
He grants me peace
in a troubled world.
He is my refuge and strength
through difficult times.
He renews my hope
for the future.
I will rejoice when
I gaze upon His glorious face.
My wonderful Lord and Saviour!

## God, My Comforter

When my son, David, was a couple days away from his 6th birthday, he fell ill. I rushed him to emergency in our local hospital. He was then transferred by ambulance to a hospital in the city. What a frightening time. As we were travelling in the ambulance to the city hospital, the words from "God, My Comforter" which I had just written a couple of weeks before this happened, kept going through my mind. I realized then that God gave me these words to help me through this difficult time. He was preparing me for this. I thank God for being my strength and comforter. I praise God for healing David. When you are going through a difficult time, give it all to God and He will be your refuge and strength. He is a God of power and hope. The outcome may not always be good, but we can rest in the assurance that God is always there to be our Comforter in our time of need.

*"Don't be afraid, for I am with you. Don't be discouraged, for I am your God. I will strengthen you and help you. I will hold you up with my victorious right hand."*

Isaiah 41:10

*"We can rejoice, too, when we run into problems and trials, for we know that they help us develop endurance. And endurance develops strength of character, and character strengthens our confident hope of salvation. And this hope will not lead to disappointment. For we know how dearly God loves us, because He has given us the Holy Spirit to fill our hearts with His love."*
Romans 5:3-5

*"God blesses those who patiently endure testing and temptation. Afterward they will receive the crown of life that God has promised to those who love Him."*

James 1:12

21

# GOD'S PROMISE

In the midst of the storm,
mighty winds howl.
Clouds drift endlessly across
the darkened sky.
Sheets of rain fall.

But, once again,
the clouds open up.
Sun's radiance
filters through.
Glorious light shines down.
Raindrops sprinkle the beautiful roses.

A majestic rainbow reaches across

the darkened sky.
Its array of colours
reminds me
of God's promise.
He protects me
in the palms of His hands.
The bluebird sent by God
perches outside my window,
softly singing the assurance,
God is always with me.

Sheltered in His everlasting arms.
God promises me,
"I will never leave you
nor forsake you."

## God's Promise

Many years ago, one of my uncles was diagnosed with bone marrow cancer. He suffered greatly with it. He was not a church goer, but he knew the love of God. I thought about him and prayed for him many times. One day, God whispered words to me which became this poem. Uncle Murray loved nature, flowers, birds-all of God's creation. He framed this poem and hung it on a wall in his "quiet" room. He expressed to me the love he had for these words which he knew God had given to me for him to ponder. He would read these words every day and he knew the Lord was with him through it all. What a comforting thought for me to realize how much the words meant to him. God is always in the midst of the storm. He may not always calm the storm, but He will hold us steadfastly through it if we lean on Him. He shelters us in His everlasting arms. God will keep hold of His promise, "I will never leave you nor forsake you." Uncle Murray believed God's promise and is now Home with his Lord and Saviour.

*"This is My command-*
*be strong and courageous!*
*Do not be afraid or discouraged.*
*For the Lord your God*
*is with you wherever you go."*

Joshua 1:9

Part V

# STEADFAST FAITHFULNESS

22

# THE EVER-FLOWING RIVER

Lifting my face,
gazing at
the Heavens,
feeling
the gentle breeze
caress me.
Warmth encompassing me.
Feeling His touch,
I am alone but not alone.

Beyond rustling,
golden leaves,
the tranquil river is
ever-flowing.

Gazing upon
its serenity,
drawing me nearer.
Feeling His pull,
I am alone but not alone.

Standing transfixed by
the river's edge.
Staring in
the calm waters.
Gazing at reflections of
darkened clouds
drifting endlessly by.
Feeling His power,
I am alone but not alone.

Lingering, amazed,
watching the river
accept its challenges.
Not defeated.
Trials try to block
its path but
the water is ever-flowing.
Feeling His comfort,
I am alone but not alone.

Marveling
at the sight.
Even in times
of adversity,

the river rushes on.
Rough edges of rocks
made smooth.
Feeling His greatness,
I am alone but not alone.

He is here!

## The Ever-Flowing River

As life drifts by, I am confronted with challenges as is everyone at different times in their lives. Everyone has dealt with emotional, spiritual and physical disabilities. During these times, I pray for God's help and feel the nearness of Him. Just close your eyes and imagine yourself standing on a riverbank and feeling the gentle breeze and the tranquility of a beautiful river. So serene. Do you feel God's presence? I have been drawn to a river and have noted debris, rocks and fallen trees in the river. I noticed that the water faced challenges, but it was not defeated. It rerouted itself and went around its obstacles and kept flowing. The river, as is our lives, is ever flowing because of the grace of God. Face it, we all have rough edges. As life continues on, our rough edges are made smooth because of God's faithfulness. We are to accept the difficulties and challenges we face in life and keep going because they will make us smoother and stronger. He gives us wisdom and strength to succeed in all He wills us to accomplish. We simply just have to ask Him and we will receive it. We are never alone. God is always with us through every aspect of our lives if we are willing to put our faith and trust in Him.

*"I still belong to You; You hold my right hand. You guide me with your counsel, leading me to a glorious destiny. Whom have I in heaven but You? I desire You more than anything on earth. My health may fail, and my spirit may grow weak, but God remains the strength of my heart; He is mine forever...how good it is to be near God! I have made the Sovereign Lord my shelter, and I will tell everyone about the wonderful things You do."*

Psalm 73: 23-28

## 23

# BY FAITH

By faith,
I hear God's powerful voice
instructing me.
I listen to His plan for my life.

By faith,
I reach out as God takes me by the hand
leading me.
I walk with Him along life's path.

By faith,
God moves mountains,
restores sight to the blind,
makes the lame to walk.

God heals the sick and broken-hearted.

By faith,
God broke down the walls of Jericho,
parted the Red Sea,
delivered the Israelites.
God calms the waters in the fiercest storm.

By faith,
I believe the powerful word of God
trusting in Him.
I rejoice in His abundant love.

By faith,
I cherish the knowledge that
through His grace, love and mercy,
God will fulfill His promises for me.

## By Faith

Has your faith ever been tested? You are probably thinking "of course it has, hasn't everyone's faith been tested?" Yes, everybody's faith has been challenged at one point or another. Do you try to be your own problem solver? I know I have. I torture myself with trying to find the right solution, but then I see the Light. God is the answer to all my problems. I just need to close my eyes and feel His presence. I need to listen to His whispered answers to my prayers. I need to have faith and trust in Him alone. He knows and hears my prayers. I need to let Him do His work in His time and in His way. It all depends on my trust in God and He needs to know how much I have put my trust and faith in Him. God has done powerful and amazing things which we cannot comprehend. We need to wait on the Lord and He will give us the strength and the wisdom through every situation. Give it all to Jesus and He will see you through. By trusting and having the faith of God's will, He will fulfill His promises to each one of us.

*"This Good News tells us how God makes us right in His sight. This is accomplished from start to finish by faith. As the Scriptures say, 'It is through faith that a righteous person has life."*
Romans 1:17

*"By faith these people overthrew kingdoms, ruled with justice, and received what God had promised them. They shut the mouths of lions, quenched the flames of fire, and escaped death by the edge of the sword. Their weakness was turned to strength. They became strong in battle and put whole armies to flight."*
Hebrews 11:33,34.

24

# REFRESHED, RENEWED, RESTORED

Awakening to dawn
of a new day.
Gazing at
marvelous sunrise
above the horizon.
Gentle breeze
whispers softly.
Birds sweetly chirp
morning songs.
I am refreshed by
His Holy Spirit.

Walking with Him

throughout the day.
Turning my eyes
on Him.
Amazing is
His wondrous love.
He guides me
along life's journey.
He is by my side.
I am renewed by
His Holy Spirit.

Growing weary at dusk
at end of day.
Gazing at
the beautiful sunset
along the horizon.
Reflect on His
goodness and mercy.
He provides me with
hope and strength.
I am restored by
His Holy Spirit.

## Refreshed, Renewed and Restored

Have you ever thought about the cycle of life? I have and I'm sure you have as well. Especially at those sad moments when we lose someone we love. We meditate and reminisce about their life contemplating on their dreams, desires and accomplishments.

During these times, I pause and think about my life. Am I following my dreams, succeeding in the desires of my heart? Am I living with the knowledge of God's purpose for me? Am I pleasing in His sight? In the sunrise, the beginning of my existence, when God breathed life into me for His purpose is when my story commences. My birth, as was yours, is as the dawning of a new day. Imagine the sun creeping above the horizon and listening to the melodious sonnet of the birds singing. There is much rejoicing with exuberant joy! As our life's journey unfolds, we all experience trials, difficulties as well as triumphs. When I go through a difficult time, I have the assurance that God is walking by my side. God gives me, as well as you, trials to strengthen our faith in Him. God is an ever present guide to those who seek Him. In my accomplishments as in yours, I know He rejoices in our triumphs. What a wonderful realization that God is always with us if we seek Him and trust Him to guide us. God has given me and continues to give me wisdom, hope and strength for each tomorrow. He can do the same for you. In the sunset, the end of my earthly existence, as I grow weary I will thank and praise Him for refreshing, renewing and restoring His Holy Spirit in me throughout my life.

*"That is why we never give up. Though our bodies are dying, our spirits are being renewed every day. For our present troubles are small and won't last forever! So we don't look at the troubles we can see now; rather, we fix our gaze on things that cannot be seen. For the things we see now will soon be gone, but the things we cannot see will last forever."*

2 Corinthians 4:16-18

25

# FAITH IN JESUS

Greatness of
God's amazing love.
Eternal life promised
because of a merciful God
sacrificing His Son.
Bore shame,
agony,
loving unconditionally.
Redeemed through
precious blood of Jesus,
shed that day
upon the cross.
He paid the debt.
Offering those

gift of eternal life
who place their faith in Jesus.

Greatness of
God's amazing love.
Opens His arms
welcoming another angel
into his eternal home.
Walking along with Jesus.
Marveling at splendour
of God's Kingdom.
Gazing at sparkling river.
Listening to birds' melodious sonnet.
Awed at picturesque sight
stretching before him.
So rich, so full.
Praising God, the Saviour and Redeemer.
Now in Paradise
because of their faith in Jesus.

Greatness of
God's amazing love.
Embraced by His loving arms.
Comforting us with
His promise of eternal home.
Seeing our sorrow,
He gives strength and wisdom.
His marvelous grace
comforts with knowledge of
being reunited

with our loved one.
Walking beside still waters.
Race triumphantly finished.
What a glorious day
when we will be in Paradise
because of our faith in Jesus.

## Faith in Jesus

Have you ever thought about the end of your time on this earth? I have reflected on the concept and I'm sure you have as well. Do you reminisce about what you have accomplished? Do you dwell on your failures and wonder if you had only lived life differently? Do you anticipate on where you will be spending eternity? Does peace fill your absolute being and satisfy your soul? The knowledge of walking with our Redeemer and Deliverer; the Sacrificial Lamb; the great I Am is overwhelming. We will sing praises to our God and King. When my father-in-law was passing away, his only request was for me to write a poem and share it at his funeral. This poem were the words God gave me. I have changed the words somewhat for this book, because I had written it more personally for his funeral. The last stanza that I wrote for his funeral was:

*Through his faith and trust in God,*
*John has left a legacy.*
*A part of him dwells in each one of you.*
*We will cherish the good memories of him forever.*
*John has finished his race triumphantly.*

The way we live our lives is a reflection of those around us. How awesome it would be if we could all leave a great legacy to be passed on to all generations. We can then say that we have finished the race triumphantly. What a joyous reunion it will be when we are once again with our loved ones and walking beside the still waters. What a glorious day that will be! Because of God's unconditional love and the sacrifice of His Son, we can live with Him in Paradise. But only if we believe on our Lord and Saviour and place our faith in Him.

*"What I am saying, dear brothers and sisters, is that our physical bodies cannot inherit the Kingdom of God. These dying bodies cannot inherit what will last forever. But let me reveal to you a wonderful secret. We will not all die, but we will all be transformed! It will happen in a moment, in the blink of an eye, when the last trumpet is blown. For when the trumpet sounds, those who have died will be raised to live forever. And we who are living will also be transformed. For our dying bodies must be transformed into bodies that will never die; our mortal bodies must be transformed into immortal bodies. Then, when our dying bodies have been transformed into bodies that will never die, this Scripture will be fulfilled: 'Death is swallowed up in victory. O death, where is your victory? O death, where is your sting?' For sin is the sting that results in death, and the law gives sin its power. But thank God! He gives us victory over sin and death through our Lord Jesus Christ. So, my dear brothers and sisters, be strong and immovable. Always work enthusiastically for the Lord, for you know that nothing you do for the Lord is ever useless."*

1 Corinthians 15:50-58

Part VI

# FULFILLING HIS PURPOSE

26

# FILL ME, USE ME, LEAD ME

O Lord, how majestic is Your name.
The power of Your love
provides me with purpose.
Fall on me, Holy Spirit.
Fill me, Lord.

O Lord, my eyes focus on goal.
Joy fills my heart.
Grant me wisdom and strength
accomplishing Your purpose.
Use me, Lord.

O Lord, I am joyfully pressing onwards.
Passion fills my soul.

Your Spirit leads me on
empowering me to finish race triumphantly.
Lead me, Lord.

## Fill Me, Use Me, Lead Me

The power of God's love is amazing. He fills us with His Holy Spirit and gives us a purpose. God grants each one of us a gift. To some, He has given the gift of teaching, to some the gift of healing, to some discipleship, to some ministering, to some music, etc. People tell me that God has given me the gift of writing. I admit, I was never a good student in English. It was always a struggle. I feel that God, through His Holy Spirit, has whispered words of wisdom to help me through different times in my life. Eventually, I decided it was time to "wait" on the Lord, pray and write down those "whispered" words. A poem would then be created. The words were not always what I thought was going to be on paper, but they were the words which the Lord wanted to have me read. I realized a few years later that God was giving me these "poems" for a reason. I was not to just keep them to myself, but He wanted me to have others read them so they may also be encouraged. God gave me a purpose, a reason, for my existence. He empowered me with the desire to fulfill my passion. He gave me the wisdom and the knowledge to lead me in the right direction. Open your eyes and mind to the gift God has granted you. May you pray the words, "Fill me, use me, lead me Lord."

"*...take off every weight that slows us down, especially the sin that so* *easily trips us up. And let us run with endurance the race God has set before us. We do this by keeping our eyes on Jesus, the champion who initiates and perfects our faith. Because of the joy awaiting Him, He endured the cross, disregarding its shame..."*

Hebrews 12:1-2

27

# GARDEN OF LIFE

My life,
I commit to You.
Tending to
garden of life.
Planting seeds,
in richness
of Your soil.
Nourishing sprouts
by Your Holy Spirit.
Providing them
with rains
of Living Water.
Directing them,
to stand alone

in the Truth.
Guiding them
to the rays
of Your Light.
Cultivating them,
from evils
of this world.
Filling plants
with Your
abundant goodness.
May the yield be plenty
at time of harvest.

## Garden of Life

When I was a young child, every night my parents read the bible to me and my siblings. We enjoyed having discussions about the reading. I was 10 years old when my mother led me to the Lord. I remember it distinctly. What an awesome experience. God truly blessed me with a great family. Whenever someone opens their heart to the Lord and accepts the knowledge of Jesus as their Saviour, there is much rejoicing in Heaven and on earth. But, we are not to have it end there. We are to become disciples and reach out to others. God has commissioned us, as His children, to go forth and spread the good news. I admit there are times when I am not being Christ like and I am unworthy to be a disciple. At those times, I confess my sins and repent. And God, because of His grace and mercy, forgives me and grants me the strength and wisdom to continue discipleship. I enjoy gardening and when

I plant the seeds, it is my responsibility to nourish the plants with fertilizer and water. Also, I need to cultivate and keep the weeds away from destroying the plants. It is my task to help the plants grow strong and be well rooted in rich soil. God has commissioned His followers to be witnesses in this world. As gardeners look after their seeds, so we as disciples of Christ are accountable to help look after God's "seeds". Give nourishment and love to the "seeds" and observe them growing strong in the Truth and Light. May there be much rejoicing at harvest time because of the abundant yield from life's garden.

*"Their responsibility is to equip God's people to do His work and build up the church, the body of Christ. This will continue until we all come to such unity in our faith and knowledge of God's Son that we will be mature in the Lord, measuring up to the full and complete standard of Christ."*
Ephesians 4:12-13

*"Oh, that we might know the Lord! Let us press on to know Him. He will respond to us as surely as the arrival of dawn or the coming of rains in early spring."*
Hosea 6:3

## 28

# DETOURS

Driving down the
road of life.
Smoothly, coasting along.
Expect bumps,
bends and curves,
valleys,
hills to climb.
Fast pace and
slower speeds.
All is well.
Unexpectedly,
suddenly,
road block.
Detour!

For life's detours,
God has a reason,
a purpose.
Accept willingly,
giving God control.
He holds the reins.
Guiding,
instructing me.
Granting me
knowledge,
to find my way.
Leading me
to the expected route.
A detour ends!

In life's detours,
God has a reason,
a purpose.
Sometimes in God's plan
He uses me for
someone in need.
He opens the door
during their time of
darkness, uncertainty.
Granting me
mercy, love and strength.
Leading them
to the expected route.
Another detour ends!

## Detours

Remember the times when you have been driving down the road. You are enjoying the scenery. It's "easy sailing" and everything is going as planned and then it happens. Up ahead, you see the dreaded sign-"Detour". You wonder as to how much longer it will take you to get to your destination. You then grudgingly take the detour. But you realize, it isn't as bad as it seemed. Amazingly it all worked out better in the end. As it is in life. You think you have your life all planned out or at least you have the day scheduled and then it all changes. Remember God places circumstances and people in our lives to fulfill His plan. We might think we are driving along the right path in life, but God in His wisdom and power has the knowledge of when and where we are to be in our life. He may be the One who has placed the detour sign along our route in life for us to slow down and sense His Spirit, listen to His voice and be guided by Him. God in His great mercy reaches out to those who are in need. He also places us in our "neighbour's" pathway to help those who are lost, depressed or hurting whether it be emotionally, physically or spiritually. But you must also remember that in God's plan, you may be that someone in need and God has placed the detour signs for your "neighbour" to follow the pathway which He has planned for their life and for yours. God has our lives all planned and He promises to always be with us. Accept the detours in your life and He will guide you through.

*"Trust in the Lord with all your heart, do not depend on your own*

*understanding. Seek His will in all you do, and He will show you which path to take."*

Proverbs 3:5-6

*"The Lord says, "I will guide you along the best pathway for your life. I will advise you and watch over you."*

Psalm 32:8

29

# LEGACY

My life.
Your life.
Each one,
a small particle;
a tiny pebble
tossed
into ocean;
a huge,
clear,
shimmering
mirror.
Creating
a splash,
causing ripples;

effecting lives
outward and
beyond;
from point
of contact,
me,
you
tiny pebbles;
small particles.
Significant.
Your life.
My life.

## Legacy

My dad passed from this life into his eternal home peacefully on June 15th, 2015. At the time of his passing, I had not yet completed this book. God had whispered the words of this poem to me and I didn't realize at the time why. I know now that they were to be the last "psalms and prayers" that I would write before my dad passed away. These are the words which we should all live by with the knowledge that we are here for a purpose. Our words and actions will impact every life which surrounds us. In everything we do, we cause a ripple effect. We have all heard the famous saying, "pay it forward". When someone does a good deed or acts kindly toward another, we should then, in turn, perform an act of kindness or encourage someone with gentle words of compassion or thoughtfulness. Dad was always interested and enjoyed my "psalms and prayers." He was a wonderful and caring man. He was quiet and had a gentle demeanour; always standing firm and steadfast in his faith. Dad never complained even in the toughest of times. Everyone who met him loved him. Dad was a small being, a small pebble in this life, but he made a huge impact in the life of his family and friends. He was always interested in each one of his family's lives. Dad cheered from the sidelines and rejoiced with us in our triumphs. He wept with us when we were hurting. His life has effected lives outward and beyond the impact of his birth. God has truly blessed us with the life of my dad. Dad suffered physically at the end, but he never complained. We can rejoice, because we know that he is now free from pain and is at peace with his Heavenly Father. Dad is walking beside the still waters in the presence of his Lord and Saviour. His spirit will live on forever in each one of us. Dad finished his race triumphantly and has rewarded us with leaving behind a great legacy. May our lives also cause a ripple effect reaching outward and beyond with acts of kindness and thoughtfulness. We are to live as God has commanded us to live by loving and encouraging one another; weeping with those who weep; lending a helping hand; living as Christ is in and through us. If we place our faith and trust in God, He will be at the gates of our heavenly home welcoming us with open arms as we finish our race triumphantly saying "Well done, good and faithful servant". That is the greatest legacy someone can leave behind.

*"Well done, My good and faithful servant."*

Matthew 25:21

Part VII

# UNWORTHINESS PARDONED

30

# THE WEDDING FEAST

God announces His invitation.
He proclaims,
the wedding feast is near.
All are welcome to attend.
God stretches out His arms
for all to come.
His desire is to pour out
abundant blessings.
God promises
joy, grace and mercy,
but only to those
who willingly accepts Him.
God proclaims
in His invitation to

the wedding feast of the Lamb,
You must prepare yourself.

I am elated,
But I feel,
no, I am unworthy.
But through His grace,
He has transformed me.
God has delivered me
from brokenness and despair
into everlasting joy.
Through the experiences
God has given to me,
He has brought me
From where I was to where
He wants me to be.
Because of His invitation to
The wedding feast of the Lamb,
I must prepare myself.

The time is at hand.
God holds
the wedding garment up.
He spreads it open for me
in all my brokenness.
But because of my
willingness and acceptance,
because of my
faith in Him,
God places the garment

over my shoulders.
Because of God's grace,
the garment of righteousness
is freely given.
The wedding feast of the Lamb
has come for all those prepared.

## The Wedding Feast

How exciting it is to receive a wedding invitation. We consider it an honour and a privilege to be invited. Preparations have started for a very important time in a couple's life. You think about what you are going to wear realizing you need to dress your very best. You look forward to the day with anticipation when the bride will be united as one with her bridegroom. Although the invitations to the weddings in life are important it does not compare to the proclamation of the greatest wedding ever to be held. We have been truly blessed because we have received a request to the most important wedding ever; a wedding uniting God and His bride (His church). God has invited each and every one of us even though we are not worthy of such an invitation. We are broken, guilt-ridden, and unworthy, but God asks us to prepare ourselves because He desires each and every one of us to attend. Through His guidance, redeeming power and faithfulness, God takes us from unworthiness to acceptance of His invitation. We will be dressed in our best outfit which is the garment of righteousness. God will place the garment over the shoulders of those who are prepared for the Wedding Feast of the Lamb.

*"Then the Kingdom of Heaven will be like ten bridesmaids who took their lamps and went to meet the bridegroom. Five of them were foolish, and five were wise. The five who were foolish didn't take enough olive oil for their lamps, but the other five were wise enough to take along extra oil. When the bridegroom was delayed, they all became drowsy and fell asleep. At midnight they were roused by the shout, 'Look, the bridegroom is coming! Come out and meet him!' All the bridesmaids got up and prepared their lamps. Then the five foolish ones asked the others, 'Please give us some of your oil because our lamps are going out.' But the others replied, 'We don't have enough for all of us. Go to a shop and buy some for yourselves.' But while they were gone to buy oil, the bridegroom came. Then those who were ready went in with him to the marriage feast, and the door was locked. Later, when the other five bridesmaids returned, they stood outside, calling, 'Lord! Lord! Open the door for us!' But he called back, 'Believe me, I don't know you!' 'So you, too, must keep watch! For you do not know the day or hour of My return."*

Matthew 25:1-13

*"And from the throne came a voice that said, 'Praise our God, all His servants, all who fear Him, from the least to the greatest.' Then I heard again what sounded like the shout of a vast crowd or the roar of mighty ocean waves or the crash of loud thunder. 'Praise the Lord! For the Lord our God, the Almighty reigns. Let us be glad and rejoice, and let us give honour to Him. For the time has come for the wedding feast of the Lamb, and His bride has prepared herself."*

Revelation 19:5-7

CPSIA information can be obtained
at www.ICGtesting.com
Printed in the USA
LVOW06s2126250316
480837LV00017B/38/P

9 781928 112365